# snow watch

## written by Cheryl Archer

## illustrated by Pat Cupples

Kids Can Press Ltd.
Toronto

To my children, Jenna and Cameron, who
are the sparkling snowflakes of my life

Kids Can Press Ltd. acknowledges with appreciation the assistance of the Canada
Council and the Ontario Arts Council in the production of this book.

**Canadian Cataloguing in Publication Data**

Archer, Cheryl
    Snow watch

Includes index.
ISBN 1-55074-190-X

1. Snow — Juvenile literature.  2. Snow — Experiments — Juvenile literature.
I. Cupples, Patricia.  II. Title.

QC926.37.A73 1994        j551.57'84        C94-931172-3

Kids Can Press Ltd.
29 Birch Avenue
Toronto, Ontario, Canada
M4V 1E2

Edited by Laurie Wark
Designed by Sharon Foster Design
Printed and bound in Hong Kong

94  0 9 8 7 6 5 4 3 2 1

# Contents

# The incredible journey of a snowflake

**A** snowflake that lands on your glove has just finished a journey that started with a speck of water in the clouds above you. Imagine if you could look inside a cloud and follow that journey from the very beginning.

**2.** When the cloud is colder than about -9°C (15°F), some specks of water freeze onto the bits of dust and salt, making ice crystals. Water vapour in the cloud condenses onto these tiny crystals and they become bigger snow crystals. Because of the way water molecules fit together as they freeze, snow crystals are always hexagonal or six-sided.

**1.** Inside the cloud you would see billions of tiny bits of dust and salt carried up from the land and sea by the wind. You would also see specks of water. Energy from the Sun evaporates water from the land, lakes, oceans and rivers. When this water vapour rises and meets colder air up in the sky, some of it condenses into the tiny droplets of water that make a cloud.

**3.** As the snow crystals are tossed around in the cloud, more water molecules freeze onto the crystals. When these crystals are too heavy to float in the cloud, they fall as snowflakes.

**4.** During their journey to Earth, snowflakes change many times — they smash into each other breaking off pieces and they collide and stick together. Snowflakes are also changed by the wind, by different air temperatures and by the moisture or humidity they meet.

**5.** After about 30 minutes of falling, the snowflakes land on the ground. Their journey isn't over yet because even on the ground they keep changing. Heat rising from the ground causes the outer parts of some snowflakes to turn to water vapour. This water vapour rises and recrystallizes on the arms of colder flakes, making these cold flakes larger while the other flakes get smaller and eventually disappear. The shapes of the snowflakes keep changing all winter until spring arrives and they melt to become water once again.

# Why it snows

ou've already discovered that snow falls when water is lifted up into the sky to make clouds. But how does water get into the sky?

The Sun evaporates water from lakes, ponds, rivers and oceans, turning it into water vapour. You can't see water vapour, but there is enough of it in the air to cover the Earth with almost 1 m (3 feet) of water. The warmer the air, the more water vapour it holds. When this warm moist air rises into the sky, it cools and it can't hold as much water. The water vapour then condenses back into tiny droplets of water that you see as clouds.

You can make your own cloud by breathing on a cold mirror or by breathing outside on a cold day. Invisible water vapour in your breath condenses to make a misty cloud of tiny water droplets on the mirror or in the cold air. When some of the water droplets in a cloud freeze and fall to Earth without melting — it snows.

## Making snowflakes

The first artificial snow was made accidently by an American chemist and meteorologist, Dr. Vincent Schaefer, in 1946. He put a piece of dry ice into a freezer chest, and before long this dry ice created a cloud that dropped ice crystals onto the bottom of the chest. Later that year he made snowflakes by "seeding" a cloud. He dropped crushed dry ice into the cloud from an airplane, and the ice caused water droplets to freeze instantly. Snow crystals quickly grew in the cloud and fell to the ground.

Since then dry ice, salt and silver iodide crystals have been used for cloud-seeding to change the weather. Cloud-seeding can increase rainfall in dry areas, enlarge the snow pack in mountains, reduce hail damage, scatter fog at airports and even change the electrical nature of thunderstorms.

Today, ski resorts all over the world make their own snow. Instead of seeding clouds, they use special snowmaking machines that shoot water into the air through small nozzles. This water turns to water vapour and then freezes to become snowflakes.

# Catching snowflakes

Have you ever seen two snowflakes that looked exactly the same? An American farmer nicknamed Snowflake Bentley spent 50 years studying and photographing at least 5000 snowflakes, and he didn't find any look-alikes. In 1988 an American physicist thought she had discovered two identical snowflakes. However, after closer observation tiny differences were found, and these two flakes are now said to be "almost identical."

Exact look-alikes may never be found because snowflakes are made of millions of frozen water molecules that can be arranged to make many different shapes. As well, each snowflake takes a unique journey to Earth that affects its shape. Take a close look at some snowflakes the next time it snows to see if you can find any identical, or almost identical, flakes.

**You'll need:**
a piece of black paper
a magnifying glass
a pencil and paper

**1.** Put the black paper into the freezer until it is cold.

**2.** Dress warmly before you take the magnifying glass and paper outside.

**3.** Let several snowflakes land on the black paper. Use your magnifier to take a close look at the snowflakes. What do they look like? Can you find two alike or are they all different? Do all the snowflakes have six sides? Sketch a picture of your snowflakes.

## Try this!

Catch snowflakes during different kinds of weather — try a mild day, a cold day and a windy day. How does the shape of the snowflakes compare?

## Where does it snow?

Many people in the world have never seen snow. It snows on only one-third of the Earth every year. In polar areas, snow falls all year long, but in tropical climates it snows just on the tops of very high mountains. In temperate areas, places where temperatures aren't so extreme, snow usually falls only in winter.

But you won't find snow in all these places at the same time. Why? Because winter comes to the northern part of the world in December and to the southern part of the world in June.

If you live in a place that never gets snow, you can still see snow clouds. Cirrus clouds, cold clouds that are high above the ground, are made of ice crystals and snowflakes. Look for white feathery clouds that look like horses' tails.

**Q.** Where do snowflakes dance?
**A.** At the snowball.

9

# Snowball science

**W**hy is some snow great for packing snowballs while other snow just won't stick together? The snowflakes that fall on cold days are light, powdery and dry. If you grab a handful of this snow, you'll find it doesn't stick together. But snowflakes that fall on mild days are large, fluffy and damp. This snow packs together easily, making great snowballs.

The secret ingredient that helps hold this snow together is water. Also, as you pack your snowball, the pressure you put on the snow, plus the heat from your hands, melts the crystals on the outside of the snowball. These crystals quickly refreeze and make a thin layer of ice that holds the snow together in a perfect snowball.

## Snowball thermometers

On a mild day, you can use snowballs as thermometers to find the warmest places outside.

**You'll need:**
five snowballs the same size

**1.** Put the snowballs on different surfaces outside, such as on a rock, a patch of grass, a picnic table, a sidewalk and a parked car.

**2.** Check the snowballs often. Why do they melt at such different rates?

**What's happening?**

All surfaces absorb different amounts of heat from the Sun. Because heat energy moves from warmer things to colder things, this heat is transferred to your snowballs. The surfaces that absorbed more heat will transfer more heat to the snowballs, melting them faster.

# Snowball-on-a-stick

If you bring some snowballs inside where it's warm, you can try these amazing experiments with them.

## You'll need:

a snowball (Even on very cold days you can make snowballs by bringing some snow inside to melt. After a few minutes, pack the damp snow into snowballs for these experiments.)
a pencil
a book or other heavy object

**1.** Make a snowball and stick the sharp end of the pencil through it.

**2.** Place the pencil on the kitchen counter so that the snowball hangs over the sink. Put the book on top of the pencil to hold the snowball in place. How long does it take for the first drop of water to fall from your snowball?

## What's happening?

You'll find that it takes a long time for the first drop of water to appear because it takes energy in the form of heat to melt the snow. Heat from the Sun started to melt the snow outside and, when you brought the snowball inside, the warm air continued to melt the snow. But with the snow so tightly packed, it takes a long time before there is enough meltwater to make that first drip. If you want to speed the melting up, add more heat to the snowball by placing it near a sunny window. How much faster does the snowball melt now?

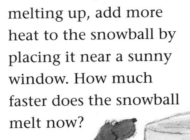

## Try this!

Put a snowball into a bowl and then into your fridge. How long does this snowball last? It takes a long time for the snowball to melt because the air in your fridge is colder than the air in your home. Heat energy from the fridge flows into the snowball at a slow rate, so the snowball melts very slowly. Put some snowballs into your freezer. They should last until next summer. Then you could throw snowballs outside on the grass.

# Snowflake shapes

**Y**ou can see snow crystals that look like stars and others that look like plates or bathroom tiles. Some snowflakes resemble six-sided pencil stubs, and some are a mixture of all these shapes. So many shapes have been discovered that they have been divided into seven basic groups. How many of these snowflakes can you find the next time it snows?

### International snow chart

Hexagonal plate

Stellar plate

Hexagonal column

Needles

Spatial dendrites

Capped columns

Irregular crystals

## Making crystals

Snowflakes are made of crystals of ice. Crystals are solids that are arranged in a regular, symmetrical pattern rather than being stuck together any old way. Some other common crystals are sugar and salt. You can make your own crystals — crystals that are good enough to eat.

**You'll need:**
250 mL (1 cup) water
a cooking pot
500 mL (2 cups) sugar
a jar
a piece of string
a pencil
a wooden spoon

1. Have an adult help you heat the water in the pot until it boils. Add the sugar, stirring until it dissolves.

**2.** Let this sugar solution cool, then pour it into the jar.

**4.** Leave the jar on the counter for a few days. Can you see crystals growing on the string?

**3.** Tie one end of the string to the middle of the pencil. Rub a little sugar onto the other end of the string and drop it into the sugar solution. Lay the pencil across the rim of the jar.

**What's happening?**

As the sugar solution cools and some of the liquid evaporates, the dissolved sugar comes out of the water or crystallizes to form sugar crystals. M-m-m-m, these crystals taste good!

# Saving snowflakes

When you catch a snowflake on your mitten, it usually melts before you get a good look at it. Scientists have found a way to catch snowflakes so they can be carried inside and studied under a microscope. You can preserve snowflakes too.

**You'll need:**

a clean microscope slide (or a small piece of thin Plexiglas)

a clean, empty plastic container with a lid (such as a yoghurt or margarine container)

a spray can of clear lacquer (from a paint or hardware store)

a magnifying glass or microscope

**1.** The next time it snows, place the slide in the plastic container and take it and the spray outside. These materials must be cooled so the snowflakes don't melt when they land on the slide.

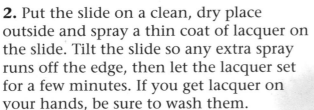

**2.** Put the slide on a clean, dry place outside and spray a thin coat of lacquer on the slide. Tilt the slide so any extra spray runs off the edge, then let the lacquer set for a few minutes. If you get lacquer on your hands, be sure to wash them.

**3.** Catch several snowflakes on the slide, then set the slide back into the container and cover it with the lid. Leave the slide outside to harden for three or four hours.

**4.** Take the slide inside and examine the snowflakes with a magnifying glass or microscope. Check the snow chart on page 12 to see what kind of snowflakes you caught.

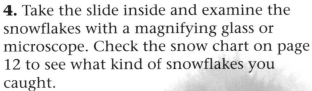

### Try this!

Do this activity on a mild day and on a cold day. What is the difference in the kind of snowflakes you catch?

## Snowflakes in summer?

Even in the hot summer, many clouds are loaded with ice crystals. But when these crystals meet the warm summer air, they melt and splash down as raindrops instead of snowflakes. If the raindrops refreeze before they land, you'll be hit by sleet.

Strong thunderstorm updrafts can toss the crystals up and down in the clouds, coating them with water droplets that freeze instantly. When these droplets are too heavy for the updrafts, they pound down as small balls of ice or hail. If you break a large hailstone apart you'll see many layers of ice inside. Hail does the most damage of any kind of precipitation. Falling at speeds of 160 km per hour (100 miles per hour), hailstones as small as peas or as large as baseballs can damage buildings and flatten crops.

# The colours of snow

You've probably heard the expression "as white as snow," but how can snowflakes that are as clear as ice look white? It has to do with the way sunlight hits the ice crystals in a snowflake. The ice crystals have millions of flat surfaces that act like tiny mirrors, bouncing back or reflecting the light from the Sun. Your eyes see this reflected light as white. Why white? Sunlight is made of a mixture of colours that combine to make white light.

You can see for yourself that snow reflects sunlight. If you live in an area where it snows, look outside on the next sunny day. Does the snow glitter like diamonds? That's the tiny ice crystals in the snow reflecting the sunlight back at you. If you look outside during a sunset or a sunrise, you might even see the snow reflecting the colours of the sky. Watch for blue, pink and even purple snow.

Sometimes when sunlight is reflected from ice crystals, it is bent, or refracted. When sunlight is bent, it is separated into all its different colours and you can see tiny flashes of colour in the snow.

# Testing reflection power

See for yourself how light is reflected from some different surfaces.

**You'll need:**
two books
a small mirror
two small pieces of white construction paper
a flashlight
a small piece of black construction paper

**1.** Use the books to prop up the mirror and one piece of white paper so they are at an angle to each other. Darken the room and shine the flashlight into the mirror. How bright is the light that reflects from the mirror onto the white paper?

**2.** Replace the mirror with the other piece of white paper and shine the flashlight onto the paper. Does the light reflect from the white paper as brightly as it did from the mirror?

**3.** Now try the black paper in place of the mirror. How well does a black surface reflect light?

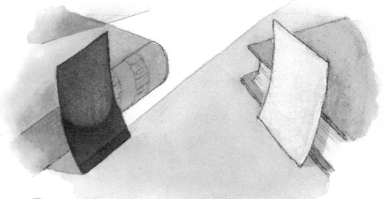

### What's happening?

You most likely found that the white surface reflected light well, but not as brightly as the mirror, and that the black surface reflected almost no light at all. Something white reflects more light than something dark because dark colours absorb light. A shiny smooth surface like a mirror reflects back almost all the light that hits it.

Snowflakes are made of crystals of ice that reflect light just like the mirror. When sunlight hits the millions of tiny crystals in the snow, the light reflected is so bright it can give you a sunburn, and it might even blind you. Snow blindness isn't permanent but it is painful. You can protect yourself by wearing sunglasses or homemade snow goggles, and don't forget your sunscreen. To make your own snow goggles, cut two thin slits in a strip of cardboard and tie it to your face with a string. The narrow slits in the goggles let you see out while they reduce the Sun's glare.

# Snow study station

You can be a snow scientist and study snow at your very own snow station.

**You'll need:**
a small area of knee-deep, undisturbed snow
a shovel
a large paintbrush
a metre (yard) stick
a thermometer
a pencil and paper
a piece of black construction paper
a magnifying glass

**1.** On a cold day, make your snow study station by placing your shovel straight down into the snow and pulling it towards you. You should have a side view or profile of the snow from top to bottom. Scoop away any loose snow.

**2.** With your paintbrush, lightly brush the snow wall up and down. Can you see layers of snow? Each layer is from a different snowfall. Measure the thickness of each layer. Can you remember the snowfalls that made these layers?

**3.** Put your thermometer on top of the snow and leave it there for about three minutes. What is the air temperature? Record this on your paper. Now record temperature readings halfway through the snow and at the bottom. Is there a difference in temperature? Where is it the warmest? the coldest?

**4.** Using your black paper and magnifying glass, take a look at the snowflakes at the top, in the middle and at the bottom of your snow wall. Do the snowflakes in the different levels look the same?

**5.** With your gloved hand, try to dig into the bottom layer of snow. Is the snow hard or easy to dig into?

### What's happening?

If it was cold outside, you most likely found that the warmest place was in the bottom layer of snow, just above the ground. This warmth comes from two places — the centre of the Earth, where it is about 6000°C (10 832°F), and from heat that was absorbed from the Sun and stored in the ground during the summer.

Because heat moves from something hot to something cold, the heat in the snow blanket rises from the ground and flows up through the cold snow. The small air pockets in the snow slow the flow of heat. Just like the blanket on your bed, the blanket of snow is an insulator — it traps heat and keeps things under it warm. Above the snow, the winds can blow and it can be very cold, but below the snow it is warm and quiet.

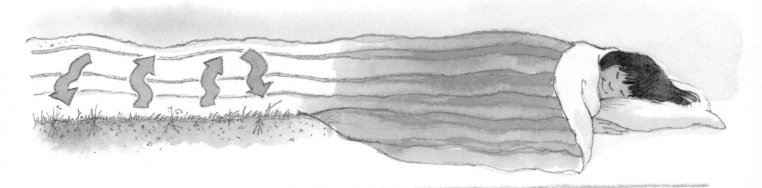

### Try this!

❋ Repeat the temperature readings on a mild day when the air temperature is above -5°C (23°F). You'll probably find it is warmer above the snow than below the snow. On mild days, heat flows from the warm air down into the cooler snow blanket, melting the snow. This is how snow melts in the spring.

❋ Make one snow study station in a wooded spot and one in the open. Are the temperature readings and the snowflakes the same at each station? Where would it be easier for plants and animals to live — in the woods or out in the open?

19

# Pukak snow

**W**hen you made your snow study station in the activity on page 18, did all the snowflakes in the different layers look the same? Chances are you found the largest crystals at the bottom of the snow. You probably also found it was easy to dig into this layer. The subarctic Indians and arctic Inuit of northern Canada, and the Eskimo in Alaska call this granular snow *pukak* (pronounced "poo-cack"). Heat that rises from the ground partly melts the bottom snowflakes and they become these pea-sized grains of snow.

If you could shrink and visit the pukak layer, you'd be surprised to see what a busy place it is. Mice, shrews and voles scurry about in the pukak layer all winter long. Under the snow blanket, these small animals are protected from predators and cold temperatures, and there are plenty of plants and seeds to eat.

Animals that use the snow blanket to survive the cold winter are called chioneuphores. Because these animals don't have special adaptations to survive the cold, they would freeze or starve if they stayed above the snow. But sometimes they have to go to the top of the snow to build tunnels or ventilator shafts for fresh air. Look for these ventilator shafts — they are holes in the snow about the size of your thumb.

## Snow words

Scientists around the world use the language of the Kobuk Valley Eskimo of Alaska when they talk about the different types of snow. How many of these kinds of snow can you find?

**Anniu** (an-nee-you) falling snow
**Api** (ah-pee) snow on the ground
**Siqoq** (see-kok) drifting snow or "snow snakes" you see blowing across the snow or along a road

**Upsik** (oop-sik) wind-packed snow
**Qali** (kal-i) snow that collects on tree branches and fence posts
**Qamaniq** (ka-man-ik) a bowl-shaped hollow in the snow around the bottom of an evergreen tree

# Looking for snow critters

You can find all kinds of interesting insects living down in the pukak snow, so grab a shovel and get digging.

**You'll need:**
a small shovel
a spoon
a clean, empty plastic container (such as a yoghurt or margarine container)
a magnifying glass
a field guide to insects

**1.** Dig down into the snow with the shovel, watching for critters.

**2.** With the spoon, collect any insects you find and put them into the plastic container.

**3.** Use the magnifying glass to look at the insects more closely, and use the field guide to help you identify them. When you are finished, return the insects to the snow.

**What to look for**
Watch for spiders, ants, beetles, mites, ticks, flies and springtails living under the snow. On warm sunny days, you might even see the springtails on top of the snow.

# Snow insulation

How can something as cold as snow trap heat? The next time it snows, collect a bowl of snow and discover the insulating ingredient inside every snowflake.

**You'll need:**
a small plastic bowl
a ruler
a pencil and paper

**1.** Place the bowl outside to catch snowflakes. When your bowl is full, bring it inside and measure the depth of the snow. Write this amount on your paper.

**2.** Let the snow melt. Now measure the depth of the water and record this measurement on your paper. Save the meltwater to test how clean your snow is in the activity on page 24.

## What's happening?

You will have much less water than you had snow — 25 cm (10 inches) of snow usually melts to make about 3 cm (1 inch) of water. What happened to the other 22 cm (9 inches)? The missing amount is air. Snowflakes are made of frozen water and spaces containing air. It is this air, trapped inside and between every snowflake, that makes snow a good insulator, because air helps to slow down heat flow. Can you think of some other insulators? Your warm winter jacket, a thermos flask and the fibreglass insulation in the walls of your home are all good insulators. Anything that has trapped air inside reduces the escape of heat.

Just as your winter jacket protects you from the cold, the insulating blanket of snow protects plants, small animals and insects from the harsh weather above the snow. It also keeps the ground from freezing to great depths, so farmers and gardeners have a longer growing season.

### Try this!

See for yourself how well the snow blanket insulates. Make some Jell-O or other flavoured gelatin following the directions on the box. Pour an equal amount of the Jell-O into two plastic containers and cover with lids. Place one container on top of the snow and bury the other container under the snow.

Check them often to see how long it takes for the Jell-O to freeze. Which one freezes first? If you were a plant or animal, where would you rather live — above or below the snow? Try this activity again, wrapping the containers with an insulating material such as a woollen scarf or a small blanket. How long does it take for the Jell-O to freeze now?

### Quiet snow

Have you ever noticed how quiet it is after a snowfall? All the sounds, even your voice, seem to be muffled by the fresh snow, because snow actually absorbs sounds. It is the tiny air spaces in fresh snow that trap the sound waves, making snow a perfect sound absorber.

# Is snow clean?

Have you ever tried to catch snowflakes on your tongue? They may melt in your mouth like a Popsicle, but how clean do you suppose they are? The next time it snows, try this activity to find out how clean your snow is.

**You'll need:**
a clean, empty plastic container with a lid
 (such as a yoghurt or margarine container)
a piece of paper towel or a coffee filter
a bowl
a magnifying glass

**1.** Collect fresh snow in the container.

**2.** When the container is full, put the lid on and bring it inside. Let the snow melt.

**3.** Hold the paper towel or filter over the empty bowl. Mix the melted snow and pour it slowly into the bowl. Can you see dirt collecting on the towel or filter? Use the magnifying glass for a closer look.

### What's happening?

Every snowflake forms on a speck of dust or salt, and as these snowflakes fall, they collect many more bits of dirt from the air. In large cities, where there is air pollution, the snowflakes pick up an amazing amount of dirt. Snowflakes might sparkle, but they sure aren't sparkling clean.

## Cleanest snow

You can find the cleanest snow at the coldest place on Earth — in Antarctica, far from large cities and pollution. Chances are this snow might even be clean enough to eat. Nero, the emperor of Rome in AD 37, ate snow as an ice treat. He had snow carried down from the mountain tops so he could eat it, mixed with honey or fruit juice.

# Acid snow

You've probably heard about acid rain, but did you know that there is acid snow, too? In some places the snow is almost as acidic as vinegar. Acid snow and rain can kill lakes and trees, harm plants and animals, spoil drinking water and destroy buildings. When acid snow melts in the spring, the acid is released into streams, rivers and lakes, killing young fish. Car exhaust is one of the causes of acid snow and rain, so ask your family to park the car and walk, cycle or take the bus whenever they can. You can measure how acidic the snow is in your area with this simple test.

**You'll need:**
purified water (not tap water)
a cooking pot
a red cabbage
a knife and cutting board
a strainer or sieve
a clean container or bowl
a small container of snow
a spoon

**1.** Have an adult help you heat 250 mL (1 cup) of purified water in the pot.

**2.** Carefully chop up one-quarter of the cabbage and add it to the pot. Let it stand in the warm water for 30 minutes.

**3.** Strain the cabbage from the water, saving the cabbage water in the clean container. Compost the cabbage.

**4.** Put a spoonful of snow into the cabbage water. Does the cabbage water turn red?

**What's happening?**
If your snow turns the cabbage water red, the snow is acidic. Acids in the snow such as sulphuric and nitric acid react with the cabbage water, turning it different shades of red. The more acidic the snow, the darker red the cabbage water becomes.

# Glaciers

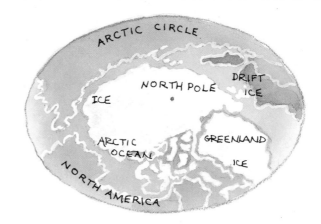

 snowflake is a lacy crystal of ice no bigger than your thumbnail. But when millions of snowflakes are packed together and start to move as a sheet of ice, you have a glacier — one of the biggest movers on Earth. Almost 11 per cent of our planet is covered by glaciers. You can see them on tall mountains all over the world or as giant sheets of ice in polar regions.

Glaciers are made as layers of snowflakes build up over time, squeezing out air and becoming dense blue crystals of ice. It is the weight of all this ice that eventually causes the crystals to glide over one another, pushing the glacier outward just like pancake batter spreading on a griddle. Another way that glaciers move is by sliding along on meltwater that forms under the ice.

## Make a mini-glacier

When a glacier moves it's like a bulldozer shaping and changing the land hidden beneath it. Make your own mini-glacier and see how powerful it can be.

### You'll need:
a metal cookie sheet
an empty plastic container (such as a
    yoghurt or margarine container)
ice cubes
waxed paper
a cup of sand

**1.** To make a mountain slope, prop up one end of the cookie sheet on the plastic container.

**2.** Rub an ice cube over the cookie sheet to make it wet, then stick a piece of waxed paper onto the cookie sheet.

**3.** Hold a fresh ice cube at the top of the cookie sheet. This is your mini-glacier. Pressing on the ice cube, push it slowly down the cookie sheet. Does it leave drops of water along the waxed paper? This water is like the thin layer of meltwater under a mountain glacier. The friction of the glacier against rock makes enough heat to melt some of the bottom ice. You won't find this water under most polar glaciers because these glaciers are so cold they are frozen to the bedrock.

**4.** Let the ice slide down the cookie sheet several times on its own. Does the ice move faster as more water droplets gather on the cookie sheet? The more meltwater a glacier has under it, the faster it moves because the water coats and lubricates the rock and reduces friction.

**5.** Sprinkle some sand on the waxed paper. Put the ice cube on top of the sand and hold it there for a few minutes. Pick up the ice cube and turn it over. Is there sand stuck to the bottom of your mini-glacier? A real glacier also picks up sand, gravel and large stones as it moves along the land. Place the ice cube, sand side down, at the top of the cookie sheet. Then, pressing on the ice cube, slide it down the cookie sheet. What changes do you see in the waxed paper?

### What's happening?

You probably found that the sand frozen to the bottom of your mini-glacier left scratches in the waxed paper. The gravel and rocks frozen to the bottom of a real glacier also erode the surface of the land by scraping and gouging it. If you could fly over some parts of Canada and the northern United States, you would see huge grooves where moving ice stripped the soil and dug deep into the rock. The ice also pushed gravel and stones into low rocky piles called moraines. You've probably driven through valleys and swum in lakes that were gouged out by glaciers. The basins of North America's Great Lakes (lakes Superior, Michigan, Huron, Erie and Ontario) were made by glaciers.

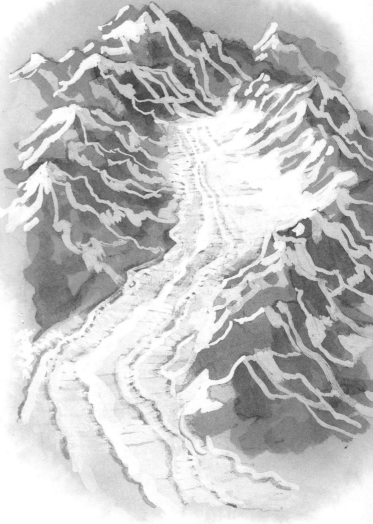

# Melting glaciers

If you're thirsty, how about getting a drink of water from a melting glacier? Cold, crystal-clear meltwater from glaciers flows through taps in many cities around the world. Glacial meltwater has actually been used for a long time by farmers to water their crops and in dams to make hydroelectric power. With all this fresh water frozen away in glacier ice, scientists have been experimenting with ways to get more meltwater from glaciers. One way is to change the amount of sunlight a glacier reflects. A glacier's white surface reflects most of the heat it receives from the Sun. If more heat were absorbed instead of reflected, the glacier would melt faster. But how can you change the surface of a glacier? On the next sunny winter day, grab some paper or cloth and head outside to see how it's done.

**You'll need:**
a piece of black paper or thin black cloth
a piece of white paper or thin white cloth
three differently coloured pieces of paper
   or cloth
some small stones

**1.** On a mild day, place all the paper or cloth pieces on the snow in full sunlight for two to three hours. Place stones on the pieces to hold them down.

**2.** What happens? Does the black piece sink into the snow deeper than the other colours? Does the white piece stay on top of the snow?

28

## What's happening?

The black piece sank the deepest into the snow because dark colours absorb more of the Sun's heat. The white piece reflects the Sun's heat, so it stays on top of the snow. This same experiment was conducted by Benjamin Franklin in 1761. What did he do with his findings? Franklin told a friend that her summer hat should be white like the snow, so it would reflect the Sun's heat.

Today, scientists have used the findings from this experiment to melt glaciers. Scientists have tried sprinkling glaciers with coal dust so that less heat is reflected and more heat is absorbed. People in China have been spreading ashes and dirt on glaciers for years to increase the amount of water that melts, but this is a messy and expensive job. In some countries, scientists have even tried to get more meltwater from glaciers by helping glaciers to grow. They put up snow fences, set off avalanches above glaciers, and seed clouds to make more snow fall on glaciers.

In Japan, scientists are trying to grow new glaciers by covering mountain snow with plastic insulation during summer. If this keeps the snow from melting, snow will pile up every winter until it becomes a glacier. These homemade glaciers could supply Japan with water during dry spells and act like giant air conditioners during heat waves.

## Too much meltwater

You can find most of the world's glacier ice in the huge ice sheets of Antarctica and Greenland. But there are another 200 000 glaciers scattered about the Earth — glaciers that hold as much water as all the world's rivers and lakes. What would happen to these glaciers if the Earth warmed up? A global warming of only a few degrees could melt glaciers and cause oceans to rise. This extra water could flood islands, coastal lowlands and cities like Vancouver, New York and Tokyo. Some scientists think the Earth is getting warmer because carbon dioxide and other gases in our atmosphere are trapping too much heat from the Sun. But we can help to prevent this global warming or greenhouse effect by driving cars less often and by planting lots of trees.

# Icebergs

When a glacier meets the ocean it creeps off the land and into the water until, with a roar, a huge chunk of ice called an iceberg breaks off and floats away. Icebergs can be the size of a dump truck or bigger than a city. The largest icebergs come from the glaciers in Antarctica, where huge flat pieces of ice break off the floating ice shelves. An iceberg as big as the country of Belgium was once spotted close to Antarctica. In the Arctic Ocean there are jagged icebergs that have broken away, or calved, from the glaciers of Greenland, Alaska and Canada's Ellesmere Island.

Where do these icebergs go? An iceberg can travel up to 13 km (8 miles) a day and last as long as ten years. As the iceberg is pushed by the wind and carried by ocean currents, it melts and breaks into smaller pieces of ice called bergy bits (house-sized pieces) and growlers (car-sized pieces). Eventually the iceberg melts and disappears into the sea.

## The tip of the iceberg

Have you ever heard the expression "that's just the tip of the iceberg?" It comes from the fact that only about one-tenth of an iceberg, or the tip, stands above the water. The rest of the iceberg floats hidden below the water. It is this hidden part that ships have to watch for because they can be far away from the tip of the iceberg and still crash into the ice below the surface.

One of the worst iceberg disasters happened in 1912, when the *Titanic*, the world's largest passenger ship, struck an iceberg and sank. After that, the International Ice Patrol was set up to find and track dangerous icebergs.

# Make a mini-iceberg

See for yourself how an iceberg floats by making a mini-iceberg.

**You'll need:**
a small, clean plastic container with a lid
   (such as a margarine or yoghurt container)
water
a freezer
a large clear bowl

**1.** Fill the small container with water to the rim, snap on the lid and put the container into the freezer until the water is frozen.

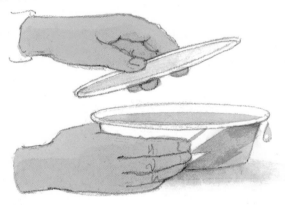

**2.** Take the container out of the freezer. What has happened to the container? Run warm water over it to loosen the ice.

**3.** Put water in the large bowl and place your mini-iceberg in it. Does the iceberg float at the top of the water? How much of it floats below the water? Can you make your iceberg sink?

## What's happening?

Even when you press down on your mini-iceberg, it rises back to float along the top of the water with about one-tenth of the ice above the water. Why doesn't it sink to the bottom of the bowl as other heavy objects would? Ice floats because, unlike other substances, water expands when it freezes — the water molecules move out into a widely spaced lattice of crystals. You saw this happen when the water expanded as it froze and changed the shape of the plastic container. It's the same thing with coins from a piggy bank — if you spread the coins on a table, they take up more space on the table than in the bank. Because the water molecules in ice are less tightly packed, ice is less dense than water and will always float at its surface.

# The ice ages

Louis Aggasiz

I f you could climb into a time machine and go back about 20 000 years, you'd see an amazing amount of ice. Almost one-third of the Earth was covered with glaciers. The last ice age ended about 10 000 years ago, when the temperatures became warmer and glaciers started to melt. Most of the glaciers we have today are leftovers from that last ice age and can be found in mountain areas or polar regions.

How do we know these ice ages actually happened? The glaciers have left behind clues. One of the first scientists to study these clues was Louis Aggasiz. When he explained to a group of scientists in 1837 that many of the large boulders in the mountains of Switzerland had been left there by glaciers, they thought he was crazy. Some people said the boulders had been left by icebergs, others thought they had been left by

Noah's flood and some even believed that witches had dropped them.

But Aggasiz had discovered that the boulders were made of granite, a kind of rock you can't find in the area, so he was certain the boulders had been moved there from somewhere else.

You can find out-of-place boulders, or erratics, all over the world. A famous erratic in Europe weighing 2721 tonnes (3000 tons) was carried by a glacier for almost 113 km (70 miles) before it was dropped where it sits today in the Swiss mountains. Other clues that prove glaciers once covered the Earth are grooved and polished bedrock, huge sand and gravel deposits, jagged mountain peaks and deep valleys.

An erratic in the Swiss mountains

A glacier at work

After the glacier

# Make a moraine

With some sand and a water-filled bag, you can show how a glacier pushes rock fragments along to make a deposit of sand and gravel called a moraine.

**You'll need:**
a plastic bag
water
a tray of dry sand
a fork

**1.** Fill the bag with water and tie it closed tightly. This is your glacier.

**2.** Level out the sand in the tray, trying not to pack it down. Place the water bag on the sand and push it along with your hand.

**3.** Take away the bag. Do you see a curved ridge of sand along the end and sides where your glacier was? This is a moraine. Whenever a glacier stops, rock fragments of all sizes are dropped, leaving deposits like this along the edges of the ice.

**4.** Put the bag back in the tray and poke it with the fork. What changes do you see in your moraine?

### What's happening?

As water flows out of the bag, some of the sand washes away, leaving channels in your moraine. This also happens to the sand and gravel deposits along real glaciers when the ice melts.

When glaciers melted during the last ice age they left behind lots of leftovers — piles of stones, gravel and sand that they had picked up as they moved across the land. In Europe and North America some of the stones in these deposits have been used for building fences, houses and even castles. The sand and gravel have also been used for making concrete and for spreading on slippery snow-packed roads. How can you use some of these ice-age leftovers? Why not start your own rock collection and find out more about the rocks in your area?

**Q.** What sheet can't be folded?

**A.** A sheet of ice.

# Snowstorms and blizzards

**H**as a snowstorm ever kept you snowbound or home from school? The wind can whip the snow around so wildly during a snowstorm that traffic slows to a crawl and entire cities close down. On the open prairies, farmers have even tied a rope from the house to the barn to help them find their way through the snow. These snowstorms happen because of sudden changes in wind, air pressure, temperature and humidity. But how can you tell if you're having a snowstorm or if you're having a full-blown blizzard?

You know it's a blizzard when you get lots of snow with strong winds of 40 km/hour (25 miles/hour) or more, visibility is less than 1 km (½ mile) and the storm lasts for at least six hours. When the blowing snow reduces visibility to only a few metres (several feet), you have a white-out.

Blizzards and snowstorms can sometimes surprise you. A snowstorm that hit North America in 1993 started as a tropical storm off the coast of Africa, swept across the ocean through the Caribbean Islands and then hit the eastern United States. In the States it snowed in hot places, such as Florida and Georgia, where people had seldom seen snow. The storm then headed north to New Brunswick, Canada, dropping more snow on towns and cities along the way.

## The snow eater

Have you ever heard of a chinook wind?
It can melt 60 cm (24 inches) of snow
in a day. As the chinook wind moves
up one side of a mountain, it drops its
moisture. When this dry wind flows
down the other side of the mountain,
it warms up and moves across the land,
melting or eating all the snow in its path.

# Make a snow gauge

The heaviest snowfalls happen where the temperature is just below freezing. This is the type of weather that major North American cities such as Toronto, Montreal, Detroit and Chicago have during the winter. No matter where you live or how much snow you usually receive, you'll be ready to measure the next snowfall with this simple-to-make snow gauge.

**You'll need:**
masking tape
a tall, wide-mouthed plastic container (such as an ice-cream pail)
measuring tape
a permanent felt marker
a pencil and paper

**1.** Cut a piece of masking tape about 15 cm (6 inches) long and put it on the outside of the container as shown. Measure and mark the masking tape in centimetres or inches with the felt marker.

**2.** Put this snow gauge outside in an open area where it can fill up with snow. Measure and record how much snow you get during the next snowfall. How do your snowfall results compare with the local weather report?

**3.** Check and empty your snow gauge after every snowfall, all winter long. At the end of the winter calculate the total snowfall for the season. How do your measurements compare with these record snowfalls?

❋ The greatest amount of snow to fall in one winter was 2850 cm (1122 inches) at Mt. Rainier, Washington, in 1970–71.

❋ The most snow ever recorded during a single snowstorm was at Thompson Pass, Alaska, where 445.5 cm (175 inches) of snow fell between December 26 and 31, 1955.

❋ The biggest one-day snowfall was 192.5 cm (76 inches) at Silver Lake, Colorado, on April 14, 1921.

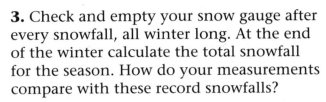

## Getting ready for snowstorms

You can prepare for blizzards and snowstorms by gathering these emergency essentials for your home and the family car.

**For your home:**
❋ extra non-perishable food, such as canned goods, crackers and nuts
❋ flashlights with working batteries
❋ matches, candles and blankets

**For the family car:**
❋ candles and matches for heat and light
❋ clean can for melting snow
❋ packages of soup and cocoa mix to add to melted snow
❋ dried fruit to eat
❋ woollen blanket or sleeping bag to keep you warm
❋ towel to wipe car windows so you can see out
❋ flashlight and flares to warn other cars
❋ shovel to dig out the car when the storm is over

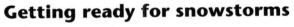
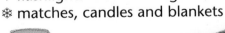

# Forecast a snowstorm

Have you ever wondered how meteorologists can forecast snow? To make a weather forecast they look at weather information that is fed into computers from satellites, weather balloons, radar stations, airplanes, ships and weather stations all over the world. But one of the best instruments for recording and forecasting weather is the barometer.

A barometer measures the pressure of the air. Even though you can't feel it, the air is always pressing down on you and this pressure changes with the weather. If you can measure the changes in the air pressure, you can predict what the weather might do. Make this simple barometer so you can predict snowstorms.

**You'll need:**
a balloon
two empty jars
three rubber bands
a drinking straw
tape
a ruler
a pencil and paper

**1.** Cut off the neck of the balloon and cut the balloon up one side as shown.

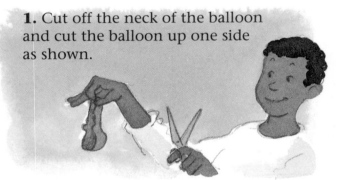

**2.** Stretch the balloon over the top of a jar and wrap two rubber bands around it, to keep it in place.

**3.** Cut one end of the straw into a point. Tape the other end of the straw on top of the stretched balloon.

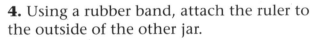

**4.** Using a rubber band, attach the ruler to the outside of the other jar.

**5.** Set the jars in a safe spot where they won't be bumped, perhaps on a counter or a shelf. Place the jars side by side so that the straw almost touches the ruler.

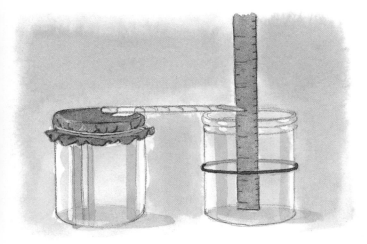

**6.** Check your barometer in the morning and again in the evening. Does the straw keep pointing to the same number on the ruler or does it move slightly? Record the number that the straw points to each day for several days. What kind of weather do you have when the straw points high? What is it like outside when the straw points low?

### What's happening?

When air pressure drops, the air inside the jar pushes the balloon up, which forces the free end of the straw down. When this happened, you likely had snow or stormy weather. Falling air pressure brings snow because air under low pressure rises and cools, making snow-filled clouds. When the air pressure increases, air presses down on the balloon and the straw moves up. Rising air pressure means you're in for fine, dry weather because air under high pressure sinks, making clear skies.

**Q.** What goes out black and comes in white?
**A.** A black cow in a snowstorm.

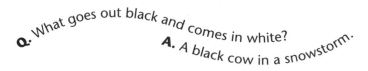

# Living in the Arctic

**C**an you imagine having snow on the ground for nine months of the year? That's what it would be like if you lived in the Arctic. This snowy place has been home for the Inuit of northern Canada, the Katladlit of Greenland, and the Eskimo of northern Alaska for thousands of years.

The ocean and land of the Arctic are also home to many different kinds of animals, such as whales, dolphins, seals, walrus, caribou, reindeer, moose and muskoxen. During the short summer, many birds live there. But the king of the Arctic is the polar bear.

This enormous bear lives in the Arctic year round and wears a three-layer coat to stay warm. When dinner time comes, the bears move out onto pieces of floating ice called pack ice to hunt for seals. If you think that sounds like slippery business, you're right, but not for polar bears — the hair they grow on the bottom of their paws gives them extra traction on the ice and snow. Their white coat also helps the bears when it comes to finding food. They cover their dark noses with a big white paw and hang out by a seal's breathing hole, blending perfectly into the snow.

## Noisy snowflakes

Have you ever walked on noisy snow? When cold ice crystals are rubbed together by your boots, they make squeaky, crunchy sounds. But this noise disappears when the temperature rises to 0°C (32°F). The warm temperature and the pressure of your weight melts some of the ice crystals, making a thin layer of water between your feet and the snow. This water coats or lubricates the top crystals, making the snow quiet to walk on.

# Snow homes

How would you like to sleep in a house made of snow? The Inuit in the Arctic and the Indians of the subarctic have modern homes with heat and running water, but when they go on hunting trips they often sleep in snow houses. The Inuit build an *igdluvigak* (called *igloo* by many people) with blocks cut from hard tundra snow.

Farther south in the subarctic, where the snow is too soft for cutting snow blocks, the Indians make a different kind of snow house called a *quinzhee*. This snow shelter is used for overnight hunting trips and can even be used as an emergency shelter during snowstorms or blizzards. If you have at least 30 cm (12 inches) of deep, soft snow you can make your own quinzhee.

**You'll need:**
a friend or adult helper
several shovels
a small shovel
a thermometer

**1.** Walk a circle in the snow about 2.5 m (8 feet) in diameter. Mix up the snow inside the circle by kicking it around with your boots.

**2.** Shovel more snow into the circle from the surrounding area, piling it into a mound about 1.5 m (5 feet) high. Round off the top of your snow pile and let it set for at least one hour.

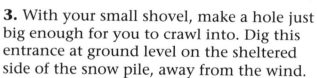

**3.** With your small shovel, make a hole just big enough for you to crawl into. Dig this entrance at ground level on the sheltered side of the snow pile, away from the wind.

**4.** Hollow out your *quinzhee* by using the small shovel to scoop out snow. As you burrow inside, make sure you clean out overhead snow. If you see light faintly glowing through the walls, stop digging so you keep the walls from becoming too thin. When you're finished digging, clean the snow off the floor to let heat from the ground flow into your *quinzhee*.

**5.** To finish your *quinzhee*, make a small hole for ventilation in the top of the roof. Now climb in, and don't worry that your *quinzhee* might fall down on you. The walls are very strong, but if they cave in, simply stand up and get out of the snow.

**6.** Take temperature readings inside and outside your *quinzhee*. No matter what the temperature is outside, your *quinzhee* will be only a few degrees below freezing because the snow walls act as insulation.

When you're finished with your *quinzhee*, just leave it. Of all the houses in the world, snow homes are the most environmentally friendly because, when winter is over, snow houses melt, leaving nothing behind.

# Antarctica

**H**ow would you like to visit a giant ice cube — one that's about 4000 m (13 000 feet) deep and is bigger than the United States and Europe placed side by side?

If you look at the bottom of a globe, you'll see there really is such a place on Earth — it's called Antarctica. It's the world's coldest and windiest continent, with average winter temperatures of -50°C (-58°F) and summer temperatures that don't get much warmer than -15°C (5°F). Brrrr! In fact, it's so cold in Antarctica that it rarely snows. Only about 5 cm (2 inches) of new snow falls every year because this cold air doesn't hold enough moisture for a lot of precipitation.

Who lives in such a cold and icy place? Scientists from all over the world live there conducting studies at research stations. Animals live in Antarctica, too, but only along the coasts and in the oceans. The blue whale, the world's largest animal, can be found there, but the most famous antarctic animal is the penguin. The penguin stays warm by wearing four layers — a layer of fat, a thick skin, an inner layer of fluffy down feathers and an outer layer of waterproof feathers. During blizzards, penguins huddle with their backs to the wind to stay warm.

Why is it so cold in the Antarctic? During summer, the Sun's rays are reflected back into the sky by the snow and ice, and in the winter the Sun doesn't shine there. For six months of the year the Antarctic, like the Arctic, is dark, and for the rest of the year it is in daylight, even at night. You can see how this works using an apple.

**You'll need:**
a chopstick, knitting needle or skewer
an apple (the Earth)
a lamp (the Sun)

**1.** Carefully push the chopstick, knitting needle or skewer through the centre of the apple.

**2.** Hold the apple beside the lamp and, tilting the apple slightly, move it slowly around the lamp. While you move the apple, keep it tilted in the same direction.

**3.** Does the lamp shine on different parts of the apple? When the top of the apple leans towards the lamp, it is always lit up while the bottom of the apple is dark. This is like the Arctic in summer and the Antarctic in winter. During the rest of the trip, the top of the apple tilts away from the light so it is dark, while the bottom of the apple is light. This is the same as the Arctic in winter and the Antarctic in summer.

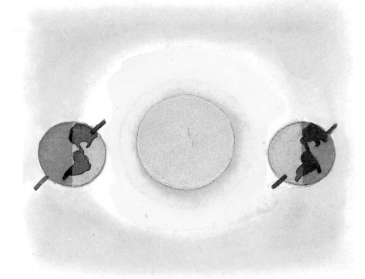

**What's happening?**

As you read this, the Earth is spinning you around at more than 800 km (500 miles) per hour. It takes 24 hours for the Earth to spin all the way around. While the Earth is spinning it also travels around the Sun, in the same way you moved your apple around the lamp. It takes one year for the Earth to get all the way around the Sun. During half of that time the top of the Earth (the Arctic) tilts towards the Sun and the bottom of the Earth (the Antarctic) leans away from the Sun, putting the Arctic in daylight and the Antarctic in darkness 24 hours a day. For the other six months of the year, the Arctic is in darkness while the Antarctic is in daylight.

# Animals in snow

**Y**ou might think that it's sometimes hard to get around in the snow, but imagine if you were a tiny animal trying to get through deep snow. Some animals, called chionophiles, have special adaptations for living in snow. These animals grow extra fur or feathers or even change their colour to match snow. There are also animals called chioneuphores that don't have snow adaptations, but manage to survive the winter by changing their behaviour. Check out this winter scene to find out how some animals cope with snow.

❄ Lynx, hare, ptarmigan and grouse grow extra hair or feathers on their feet for winter. These natural snowshoes help to spread the animal's weight over a larger area, keeping it on top of the snow instead of sinking down.

❄ Every evening ptarmigan and grouse plunge down into the snow and make a small cavity or winter bedroom called a *kieppe*. The snow protects these birds from cold temperatures, blowing snow and icy winds.

❄ Named after its large feet, the snowshoe hare can stand on its back legs to reach fresh new branches every time it snows. When the snow is deep, these hares make trails for easier travel.

❄ Burrowers like mice, shrews, moles and voles escape the cold by living in tunnels under the snow. Red squirrels are active above the snow most of the time, but when temperatures drop below -30°C (-22°F), they disappear to live below the snow.

✳ Many birds, such as the snowy owl, grow additional feathers for winter (even around their nostrils) as well as a second layer of soft down.

✳ To beat the snow and cold of winter, many birds puff up their feathers for extra insulation and huddle together on tree branches.

✳ Chioneuphores such as moose, deer, elk, wolves and fox do not have special adaptations for snow, but can survive by travelling along snow-packed trails or where snow is shallow. Moose also have long stilt-like legs that help them move through snow.

✳ Turning white in winter helps animals like ptarmigan, ermine and hares to blend in, or camouflage, with the snow and to hide from enemies or sneak up on prey. During the summer these animals are brown in colour.

## How some animals avoid snow

Some animals can't survive the snow and cold when winter arrives because snow covers their food or they just can't stay warm. These animals, called chionophobes, avoid living in the snow with some neat tricks. Some birds, bats and the monarch butterfly migrate to warmer places. Frogs and snakes head for special shelters, such as favourite ponds or rocky pits in the ground, where they hibernate. Ground squirrels and woodchucks also hibernate, while bears, skunks, chipmunks and porcupines are just very deep sleepers, sometimes waking up when temperatures are mild.

# Be a winter wildlife detective

When you walk through the snow, your tracks make a trail that tells a story about you. By looking at the tracks, someone can tell how big you are, where you were going, whether you were walking or running, and even if a friend joined you along the way.

Animals also leave behind tracks and trails. The best time to find these tracks is in winter because the snow is like a diary, recording all their comings and goings. Gather up your detective gear and head out into the snow to discover what the animals are up to in winter.

**You'll need:**
a measuring tape or ruler
a notebook and pencil

**1.** After a snowfall, visit a nearby park, or even a backyard, and look for animal tracks. (Sand also records animal tracks, so if there is no snow, visit a sandy beach early in the morning to find tracks.)

**2.** Look at the pattern of the tracks and compare it with the track patterns on the next page. Which group of tracks does your track belong to? Look at the shape of the track, the number of toes and check to see if there are claw marks. Measure the size of the track and the distance between the tracks. Record this in your notebook. What animal could it be?

**3.** Follow the tracks by walking beside them and look for other signs of activity such as a chase (tracks criss-crossing over each other), a fight (feathers, fur or blood in the snow) or signs of eating (tips of branches chewed). Are there tail marks, wing marks or any other marks in the snow? Look for an entrance to a winter home.

**4.** Now use your detective skills and your imagination to put together the clues about what your animal was up to in the snow.

# Track patterns

## Straight line of single prints

Canines (dogs, wolves), felines (cats, lynx) and ungulates (deer, moose) make this pattern in the snow when they walk or trot. Their back feet land in the tracks made by their front feet.

## Evenly spaced pairs or bunches of prints

Weasels and other animals with short legs and long bodies make this pattern in the snow by bounding forward with both feet at the same time. Birds also make tracks like these when they hop through the snow.

## Groups of four prints

Rabbits, squirrels, hares and some mice make this pattern in the snow by landing with their hind legs ahead of their front legs.

## Evenly spaced pairs of different-size tracks

Raccoons, porcupines, muskrats, beavers and other wide, heavy animals waddle through the snow and leave this pattern of track.

## Common animal tracks in snow

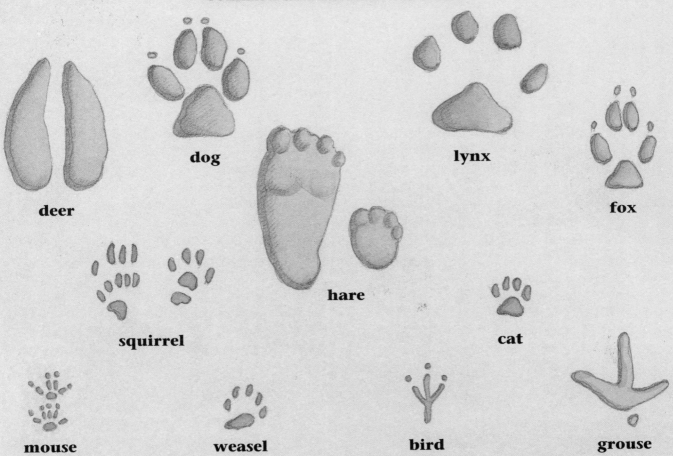

deer

dog

hare

lynx

fox

squirrel

cat

mouse

weasel

bird

grouse

# Plants in snow

**Y**ou keep warm in the winter by bundling up with more clothes, but what about plants, how do they survive the snow and cold? Many plants are helped by the snow. When snow covers plants and drifts up against tree trunks, it protects them from cold temperatures, wind and hungry animals. The snow also covers some of next year's buds, roots and bulbs, preventing them from drying out. But even with lots of snow around them, plants still freeze in the cold winter air. How do these plants prevent their cells from freezing and bursting? Make some plant antifreeze to see how plants survive the winter.

**You'll need:**
a measuring cup
water
two empty plastic containers (such as yoghurt or margarine containers)
sugar
a spoon
masking tape and a pencil
a freezer

**1.** Measure 250 mL (1 cup) of water into each plastic container.

**2.** Mix two spoonfuls of sugar into one of the containers. Use the tape and the pencil to mark this container as the plant antifreeze.

**Q.** What is ploughed but never planted?
**A.** Snow.

**3.** Place both the containers in the freezer. Check the containers every hour or so. Does the sugar water freeze?

### What's happening?

The sugar water does not freeze solid, as the plain water does, because adding sugar to the water lowered its freezing point of 0°C (32°F). That's how plants keep their cells from freezing and bursting. In late summer plants add more sugar to their fluids, but this antifreeze is only good to about -10°C (-23°F). To protect their cells from freezing and bursting at lower temperatures, plants move water out of their cells. The area around the cells may freeze, but the actual cells are not damaged.

Frogs, toads and many insects make a similar kind of antifreeze to prevent the tissues in their bodies from freezing.

## Losing leaves

Did you know that winter is like a desert for plants? Even though there is water all around them, it is frozen as snow or ice and the plants can't use it. In winter, plants and trees slow down and stop growing, so they don't need much water. When this happens, plants don't need their food-producing leaves, so they drop them. Only evergreens, such as pine trees, keep their leaves all winter because moisture is not lost through their small, waxy needles.

# Acknowledgements

I thank my lucky stars to have had such wonderful assistance from so many talented people as I wrote this book. I am grateful to Dr. William Pruitt (alias The Snow Man) at the University of Manitoba and Dr. Tim Ball at the University of Winnipeg for sharing their vast knowledge on snow and for reviewing the manuscript for scientific accuracy. I appreciate the professional advice and assistance from Ken Porteous of Manitoba Provincial Parks Branch who reviewed the manuscript with his daughter Lindsay Rose. A big thanks to Ken for introducing me to the many wonders of snow when he hired me to work as park naturalist at Birds Hill Provincial Park in the 1980s. Thanks also to the following people who helped me find a huge supply of research material: Lorraine Douglas and her staff at the Winnipeg Public Library, Corrine Tellier at Library Media Services, Paulette Patenaude at Neil Campbell School and Nancy Bremner at Birds Hill Park. Other consultants who enthusiastically responded to my many questions were Dr. Isabel Waters and Dr. Anni Scoot at the University of Manitoba and the staff at Environment Canada. Thank you all!

I am especially indebted to Lowell Campbell, my father, who with his engineering background, computer wizardry, extensive home library, love of the environment and amazing understanding of science assisted me many, many times during the research and writing of this book. In addition, I appreciate the help and support provided by the Manitoba Arts Council and the Canadian Children's Book Centre.

I am also most grateful to the incredible staff at Kids Can Press for being so supportive and encouraging throughout the production of this book; to Laurie Wark, my editor and "wordsmith extraordinaire," who made writing this book a joy rather than a job; and to Valerie Hussey and Ricky Englander, who believed in me and made my childhood dream of being an author come true. And thank you to Pat Cupples for the brilliant illustrations that make this book "sparkle," to Sharon Foster for her wonderful design, and to Elizabeth MacLeod for her expert polishing job in the final stages of production.

And finally, a great big hug to my husband Pat for his support and enthusiastic "go for it" attitude, when I shared the idea for this book with him, one snowy January evening.

**Q.** Where do snowmen keep their money?

**A.** In snowbanks.

# Glossary

**chinook:** a warm, dry wind that blows down the side of a mountain and moves across land, melting snow in its path

**chioneuphore:** an animal that survives living in snow by changing the way it lives, such as travelling along snow-packed trails or living under the snow

**chionophile:** an animal that has special features or adaptations for living in snow, such as growing extra fur or feathers, or changing colour.

**chionophobe:** an animal that can't survive in snow and has ways to avoid snow, such as migrating or hibernating

**condensation:** the process of changing from a gas to a liquid, such as when steam changes to water droplets

**conduction:** the transfer of heat from hot objects to cold objects

**crystal:** a substance with regular, evenly-spaced flat surfaces. Snowflakes are crystals; so are salt and sugar particles.

**crystallization:** the process of forming crystals from a liquid or a gas

**erosion:** the wearing away of Earth's surface by glaciers, water, wind, etc.

**erratic:** a large rock carried a distance by a glacier

**evaporation:** the process of changing from a liquid to a gas or vapour, such as when water boils and becomes steam

**glacier:** a large mass of ice moving slowly down a slope or across land

**greenhouse effect:** the warming effect produced on Earth when heat from the Sun is trapped by gases in Earth's atmosphere

**Ice age:** the time period when large areas of the Earth were covered by glaciers. The last ice age ended about 10 000 years ago.

**insulator:** a material that reduces the spread of heat, electricity or sound

**meltwater:** the water produced when ice or snow melts

**meteorologist:** a scientist who studies the Earth's atmosphere, especially for making weather forecasts

**quinzhee:** a shelter made from a hollowed-out mound of snow

**reflection:** the throwing back of light, sound or heat

**refraction:** the process in which light is bent as it passes from one material to another

**solution:** a liquid with a substance dissolved in it

**updraft:** an upward movement of air

**water vapour:** the invisible gas formed when water is heated

# Index

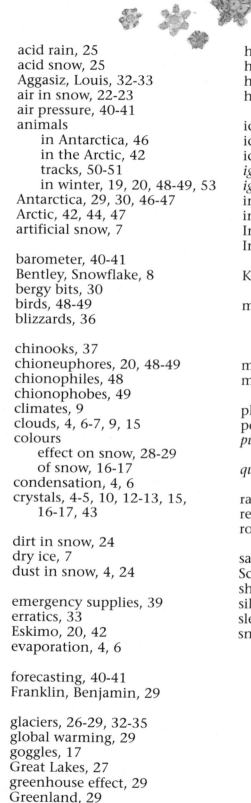
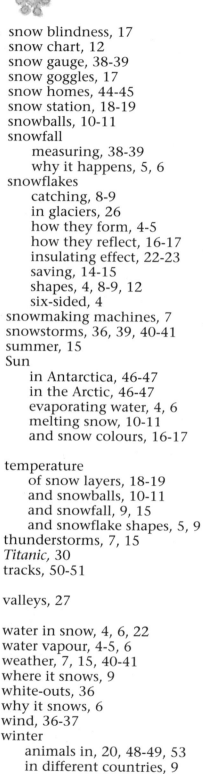